NAKED

There are poems here that I will return to again and again and poems I won't have to return to, for they will haunt and enliven me for years. For millennia, theologians have placed blame for the shame of nakedness on the shoulders of women: Thank God they've failed to scare Mutesa and Bunce off from embracing that mighty, Edenesque state of being."

— DA'SHAWN MOSLEY
editor and journalist

"This is a tender, whimsical and yet fiercely honest exploration of love, identity and personal growth illuminated by a natural world of birds, sky and sea that the poems woo us to revel in. We witness a conversation between two poets, in almost one voice, as their poems resonate in a back-and-forth rhythm of truth-searching and loving. This innovative form, the deceptively simple language, and the illustrations' clarity invite us into the very hearts, minds, and yes, bodies of the poets as they confront contradictions of race, gender, societal expectations, and more. We cannot but recognise ourselves in these 'musings'; in the journey from innocence to knowing that beckons us further into the mystery of self. An insightful and impressive debut."

— DOREEN BAINGANA,
Commonwealth Writers' Prize award winner
and author of *Tropical Fish*

NAKED:

the honest musings of 2 brown women

by Mimi Mutesa & Selvi M. Bunce

POEMS

THE **BLACK SPRING**
PRESS GROUP

First published in 2023
An Eyewear Publishing book, The Black Spring Press Group
Grantully Road, Maida Vale, London W9, United Kingdom

Typeset with graphic design by Edwin Smet
Author photographs Mimi: Jonathan Ssajjabbi / Selvi: Mimi Mutesa
Illustrations Mimi Mutesa

isbn 978-1-915406-40-8

The authors have requested American spelling and grammar be used for this book.

BLACKSPRINGPRESSGROUP.COM

Dedicated to all of us who are bad, brown, and brazen.

CONTENTS

GOLD

WE BIRDS, WE CANNOT FLY

IGNEOUS HEART

RISING MAGMA

SUN & MOON

NOTE TO THE READER

Before you dive into this book, we wanted to explain exactly why we decided to collaborate. You're about to fall into many worlds, worlds that – until we first showed each other on a rainy September day – we didn't think anyone else could understand. Poetry is an incredibly intimate and personal medium; laying your cards on the table and sharing your poetry with someone else is almost as personal as letting them read your journal. But that's exactly what we did. That's how this book was born. It was scary, beautiful, terrifying and a relief all at the same time. The moment we decided to trust each other with our work, to absorb it without caveats or excuses, we both felt incredibly seen. And while this body of work is for everyone, that was a huge moment for us as women of color. Almost immediately we knew we had to embark on this journey together, if only to open up our worlds to you so that you too might feel as seen as we did with each other that rainy day and every day after. We wrote this book together because we love community and sisterhood. There's no way we could have done this alone. We are incredibly excited for you to read it. We really hope you love it. We hope you laugh and cry and groan and squirm just as much as we did. But most importantly, we hope you or your loved ones feel seen by the vulnerability in this project. You deserve at least that much.

GOLD

GOLD

When I tan I turn gold
Not the brown of my ancestors
Nor the pink of the English
It is not a Mediterranean olive
Nor an Italian glow
I am golden
Like the jewelry my grandmother trades up in India
And brings home for every occasion
Like the chicken my father barbecues in his cement block pit
45 pieces at a time
Like the fire that burns in the camp in the north
As the stars burn brighter at my back
When I tan I turn golden
Golden like
Gold

"I CAN'T BE RACIST, MY BEST FRIEND IS INDIAN"

The elementary school I grew up in is now full of Indians
Brown skin on the playgrounds and at the whiteboards
Brown skin winning the spelling bees

Yet we will not flaunt this as diversity
We will not be amazed at the ability of the white community
To adjust so well
For there is still

Brown skin
On the white playgrounds and at the whiteboards
Brown skin
Winning the white spelling bees

Visitors at home
Abroad next door

The elementary school I grew up in is now full of Indians
Brown skin in a sea of white
Brown skin forgetting it is brown
Yet I will cheer them on

On the playgrounds and at the whiteboards
Winning the spelling bees
Because the elementary school I grew up in is now full of Indians

MY MOTHER'S SHOES

Many girls want to know their mothers as children
I do not

I do not want her pain
I do not want the cobras in her shoes in the morning
I do not want my grandmother's favoritism of my mischievous uncle
I do not want the shame of her developed body
I do not want the prying eyes of the *kulfi* sellers
Nor the prying hands of the gardening boy
I do not want the pain that my grandparents felt when she told them
Ten years later
I do not need to know my mother as a child

I know her now

MICROAGGRESSIONS

Whenever people ask me who I am,
I toss the version that's easiest to digest:
"Where are you from?"
"Uganda."
"Oh, really? I wouldn't have guessed."
Sometimes I offer a mute, obstinate smile, then
"For all intents and purposes, yes, Ugandan."

Sometimes I'm "American born, Ugandan bred,"
as if that explains anything.
Sometimes I'm "American born,
Uganda-Congo-Zimbabwe-Kenya bred,"
an unnecessarily complex response that I know
doesn't answer what they're not asking.

"So just Africa then? But why do you talk like that? Your English
sounds better than mine."

Sometimes it's "colonialism,"
sometimes it's "the private international schools I attended,"
sometimes it's a raised brow and a tired laugh,
– and the silent "it probably is" in my head.

"Where do you call home?"

It's always a lie
– everywhere, nowhere,
and I'm always too stubborn
to tell them apart.

ASSIMILATION BY DEFAULT

He said it was impressive
That I didn't sound at all
Like he expected when I said
"I'm from Uganda."

He said it was impressive
As if I wanted a gold star,
As if my life's goal
Had been to assimilate.

I SPY

Brown girl, brown girl
What do you see
I see a white boy
Looking at me

BACK (TF) UP

Your white skin?
Your white skin?
I made you feel self-conscious of your white skin?
Have you seen where you are standing?
Do you know who built your pedestal?
But you cannot step off –
Perhaps it is a cage,
So call it by its name
And do not blame me.
My anger? My anger?
My anger is unfair?
Who told you your unibrow was ugly?
Plucking my eyebrows in third grade –
Were you the first in your class to shave your legs?
How many men have left you for someone
Lighter? Brighter? Smaller?
This is not a competition.
I do not care
For the white man's burden.

20

HAS A WHITE MAN EVER THOUGHT THESE WORDS?

I'm afraid of drowning in my own power,
if only because I knew it was temporary.

I WAS AN OBSTINATE CHILD

When I was 6, my parents asked me if I would like to renounce my American citizenship so I could be Ugandan. I didn't know what that meant; all I knew is that I was the only American I knew and I didn't want to be the same as everybody else.

God knows why they listened.

CHAOTIC NEUTRAL

"Identity"
what a pestering word
for someone made up of everyone,
a persona pickpocket.

"Home"
what a sobering word
for someone that's out of air miles
but is still always running.
Which me is the real me?
I can't tell anymore.

Am I the ocean?
The waves constantly changing
and in doing so, perpetuating my essence?
Am I so far down the rabbit hole
of this existential crisis?
Is it chaotic if it's familiar?
Is it chaotic if I've mastered it?
Have I mastered it?
Does it matter?

WE BIRDS, WE CANNOT FLY

WE BIRDS

This crisp ceramic bowl sky,
awash with fading blues and creeping blush;
morning breeze nipping at me.

This bowl has the prettiest chip in the center,
a bright sliver, a crack shaped like the white of a fingernail:
the moon.

I wish I could hook my arm around her edge,
and hoist myself into the safety of her arms,
and just sleep there for a while.

Instead, I see the sparrows and her friends
flitting about, darting above;
so we penguins, we ostriches, we takahē,
beautiful as we are, notice little else:
not our envied plumage,
not our treasured eggs,
only the plain brown sparrows, mocking us
because we birds, we cannot fly.

INGROWN HAIR

There is something strange beneath my skin
telling me to build a house,
make a home,
mother children.
I am not sure how to reconcile it.
My mother was strong
and a mother after all.
My philosophy has been to spend my time
on myself and the world.
I have always thought
I could simply address the thing under my skin
when it finally crawled out.
But when my family starts guessing
who will get married first, and my father
has been saving wedding money for years,
I begin to wonder
if I will have to pluck it out.

MY TIN ROOF

He told me he often thought the world was ending
when the rain would fall on his tin roof,

echoing against the cement walls, reverberating in his ears,
drenching his bones as his skin stayed dry.

He told me he was angry when he was only given
one initial in primary school, and everyone else was given two.

But he was the only one with two at graduation:
M.S. Thirumalai unto the day he dies.

He told me he remembered the first time he witnessed bribery:
his father paid a judge to save the vegetable stand –

the vegetable stand that supports his cousin's family to this day.
He told me he remembered the first time he bribed –

already accepted into university,
he just had to find a way to get into the dorms.

He never told me he finished his first Master's degree
without ever owning a pair of shoes or trousers.

He never told me of his experimentation with atheism:
now he glorifies God with every breath and step.

He never told me how much he worried. He always told me
he did not believe in brute force and you have nothing if not your
education.

He told me he often thought the world was ending
when the rain would fall on his tin roof.

STRETCHMARKS & SUNSPOTS

The women in my family do not age well,
but there is something to be said for living life
so fully that you simply lose your mind
as you gain in years.
There is something to be admired
in the swollen ankles from climbing so high,
in the overplucked eyebrows from caring too much,
the ears hard of hearing from straining to hear
your own voice –
forgetful from memorizing
too many solutions.
I am ready to go gray
and grow old with grace,
but not too much grace –
I will ensure that I
deserve the gray.

FREEDOM

I envy the birds.
I can capture them on film
But they are still free.

HEARTH

The loveliest sound
In the middle of nowhere
Is rain on tin roofs.

LETHARGY

I get so lazy,
And the sun feels like acid
Melting through my bones.

YOUTH

Running through the fields
With soft mud between my toes,
Momma's gonna scold.

A FIGHTING SPIRIT

Let me join Fight Club
Let me jump over a cliff
Let me feel alive.

HEREDITARY

When I told my mother I wasn't feeling well,
That the bubbles in my stomach would not settle,
That the knot there kept growing tighter,
That I kept getting lost in my own mind,
She simply said
It runs in the family.

LILACS

Sometimes I make my mother so proud it is unbearable,
a conundrum uncomfortable to admit.

Sometimes she gushes to me of myself.
I sit and say nothing, it is better this way.

It's painful, her pride, the joy she finds in the little things I do –
so little, but she will treat them like a lilac bush

in the desert.
But what is worse is the fear her pride brings.

"I hope she doesn't get used to this,"
I secretly wish every time something goes right,
because I know my failure is imminent.

WHO IS YOUR GREATEST CRITIC?

I got a tattoo that said "Mom" in my mother's Mother Tongue,
but I could not bring myself to tell her about it.

I wanted to write a book about my grandfather,
but was too afraid to ask.

The truth awaits us behind a clearly marked door,
but we will not find it by walking past a doorknob

and expecting it to open like sliding glass.

IMMIGRANT MANTRA

If even I — who strayed most from the path laid out for us —
felt this surge of worry, that I had been constrained
to what was expected of me my entire life,
then what did they feel?

Are they truly so superior
that their cravings match their obligations?

Are they so lost
that they do not know the difference?

Do I simply think too much?
Perhaps they are better daughters than I.

Was the immigrant mantra
not chanted by my bedside loudly enough?

I am sorry I feel this way,
I promise the guilt is heavy.

RESOLUTIONS

In the cool darkness
of my sister's room in my parents' house,
I told myself
I would refuse to believe
what is not true.

LATE BLOOMER

When I was 4, my first kindergarten friend was Agaba,
he winked at me once.
When I was 6, my first (and only) sleepover was with the Sempa sons;
they had lots of rabbits.
When I was 13, I got kicked out of boarding school;
it's not my fault the boys dorm had the better TV.
My high school best friend's name was Mark.
My second best friend in high school was also Mark.
When I was 19, my first college friend was the Ghanaian boy
who got lost as frequently as I did.

When I was 22, I gave female friendships a shot.

WEATHER-BEATEN

These chipped rooftop tiles
Scalding hot from all the sun,
They know how I feel.

AMBITION

Fear not little one,
Greatness comes at a high price.
Let them be happy.

STRIVING

I'm a "good" kid.
So don't give me all that shit
For wanting "happy".

CONTROL

I want to mould clay.
Sounds like a blasphemous thought
To want to be God.

EVOLUTION

I'm obsessed with birds
And I'm taken by goldfish,
But not with humans.

EARLY BIRD

She hopped out of bed.
Her father hated a lazy worm.
By six thirty he was off – to work,
And so was she; back to bed that is.
She was on holiday after all.
She got out again at a more reasonable hour,
House to herself.
She put on loud music for a bit,
And danced as she brushed her teeth.
But took it off after a while.
He hated her loud music.
Earphones it always was; less conspicuous.
She went to the yard
And startled herself as she started to dance;
It felt good to throw her clumsy feet about.
She loved to dance,
But dancing was a useless hobby.
He hated useless hobbies.
They were for selfish people.
The rest of the day,
She did selfish and uncivilized things:
She stared at the sun
Till it became a blue dot,
She had ice cream for lunch,
She wrote a few poems,
Read a few novels.
She watched as much of the sunset
As she could, before she couldn't.
6 PM
Soon, she would have to slip on the ballet flats
That she needed to walk on eggshells.
Head down, beeline for the bedroom.

Eggshells only, not toes.
Ghost footsteps. Feather fingers.

I watched her go to bed,
Tuck herself in,
Hum a little tune that he couldn't hear.
I could only wonder mutely at
The magic a child could create
In her own little chiefdom,
Weighted by the misery
Of how quickly it could be snuffed out.

CROWN

It's raining
It's pouring
The lost girl
Is roaring

Raindrops slide down
Her burning eyes
She plots and plans
Her foe's demise

For you know not
The wrath she bears
And her vengeance for
The crown you wear

Trust not the strength
Of your glass tower
She carries stones
She counts the hour

You stole what's hers
She'll steal what's yours
She'll count the plunder
And take some more

You slip, you fall
And no one runs
She's at the throne
Your kingdom come

It's not raining
It's not pouring
Your wings are clipped
And now she's soaring

45

IGNEOUS HEART

IGNEOUS

You are imperfect yet you will not leave my mind
We were never good together
We were great together
Our chemistry
Was deniable to no one
But it was the kind of chemistry that breaks under pressure
The kind of rock that doesn't crack but simply
Explodes
We were so afraid
You and I
We were the earth afraid of itself

NO FLOWERS PLEASE

No one ever stops to think
about the act of giving flowers.
And neither did I, to be quite honest,
in our quiet minutes, hours.

But now I've firmly decided –
and there's no going back on this –
to do away with senseless murder
and never visit the florist.

Don't hand me dying flowers
in an effort to say you love me.
Don't give me decapitated roses,
and wilting beheaded lilies.

Give me seeds of love instead,
and a garden in which to plant them,
and on every Valentine's Day, make love to me
in our very own personal Eden.

YOUR PERSONAL GARDEN

Kiss the thin branches
      Of my wrists
Kiss the pale petals
      Of my eyelids
Kiss the places in my hair
      That the sun just kissed
And if each kiss be a seed
      Let them bloom
And turn me into your own
      Personal garden

EVERGREEN

I may not be your
Cup of tea
    For the first day or two
    Or three,
But moss, for me,
Is more lovely:
    For I may grow on you.

INTIMIDATING LOVE

Don't you feel so small
Looking at the vast blue sky?
You are my blue sky.

SOULMATES

We match, you and I:
Denim souls, leather heartbeats,
Machine gun laughter.

FRIENDSHIP

Don't simplify us,
Friendship is miraculous.
We're more than "just" friends.

INFATUATION

Everything is red.
Love takes things out of focus.
Where are my glasses?

AND THAT WAS JUST THE TUESDAYS

We'd scamper around the shoulder height grass,
And swim upstream the rivers.
We'd throw our clothes on the sandy banks,
And let our ten year old bodies shiver.

Now it's our lips that timidly scamper
As the moonlight beams her rays
At the pair beneath, with their whispered laughter,
That fell in love on Tuesdays.

ART SHOW

Let's show the world our bruises.
Show me the deep purple,
Like a bruised overly ripe avocado:
The colors on the skin of your lower lip
That I never thought my mouth
Would find the strength to leave.

I'll show you the maroon blotches,
Carelessly strewn around,
Scattered over the slope of my neck,
Between my thighs, and in my opinion,
Finished all too soon.
This must only be the interlude.

And together, let's show them
That the Picasso evidence
Of our drunken nights is always beautiful;
That bruises, with the purples
And reds of a glorious sunset,
Our bruises, are made with love.

CHARM OFFENSIVE

You stride into the room
late
and I am swept off my feet.

Your confidence, in spite of your blush,
captures a subtle attention that cannot be denied.
Gliding into your seat, you answer the question
you were supposed to forget,
pass when you were supposed to fail.

What I envy and love
is your ability to be natural
and succeed.
My admiration of drive has brought me here
to you;
for what you lack in practice,
you make up for in poise.

A CIRCLE IS ROUND

I will tell you what will happen
You will fall for me (if you have not already)
I will resist you
This will turn you on
I will note your determination
I will give you a chance
We will dance
You will fall harder
I will begin to fall
And as I do, I will swoop myself up and leave you
I will realize you are too much of a risk
You will cry
I will deny you
You will continue to try
I will lie
And say we are friends
You will find someone else
She will not allow you to see me

GRAND OPERA

In an empty room
This silence has a sound,
It could fill up an opera room
And leave the maestro fatigued.
It is crushing my eardrums inward
And my spine outward.

Your hand brushes mine
With the force of colliding tsunami waves.

You take it
As gently as a feather,
As gently as the tilting axis.

Your thumb,
Stirring the skin on the back
Of a hand I should know so well.
"What are you worming your way towards?"

You go over my knuckles,
Inaudibly quick.
"Are you *trying* to shatter my bones?"

You rub again,
I look up.
"You just wiped out a village
On the other side of the globe."

The crescendo is creeping.
Who turned up the volume,
It's too quiet!
Crescendo, Crescendo.

You hold my hand,
Envelop it with the other.
"You just brought a country to its knees,"
To the soundtrack of an empty room.

ADORATION

Count the stars for me,
The ones inside of your eyes.
Go blind like I did.

DEFENSELESS

Chisel to the chest,
Love till my heart breaks open,
Till I stop running.

IF I WERE A SEA, I'D BE THE DEAD SEA

I'm always salty,
A buoyant disinfectant,
You'll always love me.

GUILTY PLEASURES

My bed is monstrous,
Holding me against my will,
My miniscule will.

UNREQUITED

Romantic love unfulfilled is painful
Tortuous
The love of a friend unreturned is
Exhausting
Deadly

FASHION SHOW

hands on my body
on my clothes
the excitement of something hidden
a secret waiting to be told

fingers through belt loops
promises of power and strength
knuckles graze my stomach
testing the softness of my cashmere
whispering
gentleness and care

open windows in kitchens
closed doors in bars

something about the rush
always left me where I felt safest

wanting

FANTASY

In truth, it is all too easy to be a dream girl –
the difficult part is wondering when they will wake up.

WOULD YOU LISTEN TO A SONNET ABOUT YOURSELF?

I want to write about you,
But am unsure of the best way to go about it.
I want to sing songs of your sweet heart,
Write odes to your quiet mind,
Devote ballads to your confident fragility.
It is all so beautiful
Without being overwhelming.
But you are too humble to listen
To a sonnet about yourself.
So this is where I am,
Surely unsure.

LOVE AT FIRST RÉSUMÉ

Defining love by profession;
"Love at first résumé" my mother used to say.

I work well with finance guys,
engineers are a dream
but are altogether too soft.
The political scientists are either too driven
or not enough.
History is a bore.
I've never met a math man.

Tell me –
pragmatic or callous?

TOO FACED

In the cool tropical air, he told me he loved me. That's why I was angry. He gave it away and took it back like it meant nothing. Like he could love me like he loved the Caribbean rum.

How was I supposed to decipher what was real – how was I supposed to decide how to act with the next one, if the one thing I had somehow managed to trust had been a lie?

It was always a balance. Do not be too nice, too open, too guarded. Smile, but don't flirt.

But if he, the one who had been so real and made me feel at home, could lie with such ease, how could anyone be trusted at all?

My parents' marriage was good. I had never been cheated on. (Sure a few heartbreaks, but nothing to write a novel about.)

So I smiled. Accepted, and smiled, and laughed. But not too much, and not too loud.

SELF-SABOTAGE

Sometimes I plant things upside down.
Grow — I dare you.
Unable to handle the bloom,
rain falls and there are no roots,
but —
I planted, didn't I?

ABC, MY, OH, ME

I did not sign up for this,
This mess of knots inside of me.
We said we'd just be friends:
As simple as A, B, C.
It had been years,
We'd both moved on.
All traces of the past
Should long be gone.
But whenever I saw you
It wasn't a stray butterfly or two,
It was as if my insides
Were suddenly an entire zoo.

THE BECKONING

You finally called for me and I
Put you on hold
Just to see if you could appreciate
The elevator music.

HOW MIGHTY IS THE JUNGLE?

Sleeping alone in the same bed
we wandered for hours.

COMMITMENT

I will never have
Something borrowed, something blue,
Because I am addicted
To something new.

EXPECTATIONS

On the topic of his optimism:
isn't it better to have lowered your expectations
to protect your heart from being shattered into a million pieces?
But perhaps his heart just wouldn't shatter at all the things mine
would.

JEOPARDY

I am not sure if you
Underestimated me
Or simply forgot to estimate me at all
But I am much more powerful
Than you imagined
Or acted like you knew
You will not make the same mistake again
You will not have
The chance

LEGACY

Your next phase
Your last phase
Try something new
Before you settle down
After a heartbreak
Drink something strong
Exciting exotic
Something brave and beautiful
Something you will remember forever
Something that will make you forget
A story to tell
Go ahead
Make your friends jealous
Even your parents will fawn
No one can forget me
So while I may be your current phase
You will remember me for a lifetime

DETACHMENT

I hope it hurts you,
I hope your heart aches at the thought of me.
For I am alone by choice,
I have no longing for another man.

I love to be alone
more than I loved you.

But you,
you cannot stand it,
because you loved to be together
more than you loved me.

RETURNEE

Now you have come back
Crept into my bed
Clawed into my head
I have not welcomed you
Nor have I denied you

You were pleasantly surprised
How I love to hate that privileged
Smirk you wear

What shall I do next time?
For there shall be a next time
I like things easy

LIFE HACK

I am tired of this trope
Of being the other woman
The woman you find after a failed relationship
To change your life
To change your soul
I am not a tool to be used
I cannot change you for you
Only you can do that

I am tired of being depended on
To do everything you cannot do yourself
I need you to be strong Strong
enough to choose me
Not to need me

DOUBLE DUTCH STANDARDS

He's ignorant, but easy on the eyes.
He's an asshole, but so am I.
He's painfully awkward, I find it endearing.

She's ignorant, end of story.
She's a bitch, which makes two of us.
She's too mousy, I'm already bored.

LET ME TELL YOU SOMETHING

I responded to his claims of love and insecurity with sarcasm and
    apathy.
Misconstrued as a lack of understanding, he began his response
    with the word "understand"
and continued to explain to me the mysteries of myself in three
    sentences and with four typos.

10 SECONDS & COUNTING

alas our whirlwind
romance
is coming to an end

it seems time
has no more
of herself to lend

and you have
fewer and fewer
texts to send

MIRAGE

The intimacy we feel from knowing another's body
is addictive.
The comfort that grows is so peaceful;
it is all too easy to find yourself playing house
where no home can be built,
and buttoning shirts
when no collar will fit;
but just because two bodies fit well together
does not mean two lives will.

THE SUN SHINES IN THE DESERT

As the rose bush bloomed, you offered me everything
I told myself I wanted.

I turned, and went back into my garden
where the lilacs were dying.

ORCHIDS

I held onto our differences
Like a dead orchid
Hoping something would grow out of them
Hoping something would blossom
Our differences could be beautiful
I persevered
Watering them
Trying to maintain them
Focusing too much on the blossoms
Forgetting it is the leaves that photosynthesize

I DREW YOUR HANDS ON A PARKING TICKET

The thoughts of you
filled all the spaces of my mind:
a poem on the back of a receipt,
a sketch of your hands on a parking ticket,
both of which I knew I'd lose.

I didn't want to miss you, not again;
that's what I told myself anyway.

DISINTEGRATING PAPER

I trace our relationship by looking for the gap
In my diary where the pages do not sit quite right.

How much did I lose in those pages
I ripped out and gave to you?
Softly faded yellow,
The vine at the bottom of each page.

But I am sorry.
I took more from you
In the giving of my words
Than I lost;

For while I meant them,
I knew I would not mean them
Forever.

TIPTOES

I hold back apologies as I taught myself to do
so long ago,
whispering
that it will not work,
insisting that it cannot work.
Oh, I am sure it hurts,
but please try to understand
all that I am not saying —

I will leave you.

CYBERSPACE

The information age has heightened my spatial awareness.
Shooting messages into thin air, I suddenly
become painfully aware of the emptiness.

Do you think about me like I think about you?

The vastness.

The question echoes in my ears,
the darkness makes it impossible to hear.

Will you come back to me?

In this information age, we do not have to go anywhere to be together.
I am so much more aware of the space.

UNDER YOUR TONGUE

The word escaped your mouth so easily.
Had it been lying there all along?
Had it been curled up on the tip
Or stretched out along the ridges?
Did you feel it with every kiss,
Or tuck it under your lip like chewing tobacco?
You said it with such surety I was tempted to think
It was a defense mechanism,
But who feels the need to defend against a crying woman?
You turned away my offer of everything –
I could have given you the world
And you simply said,

"No."

But how can I be surprised?
I always knew I did not fit into your picture:
My hair, my skin, my heart
Too dark.
Yet I am surprised.
The hours we spent together were so easy,
The hours apart so hard.

INVISIBLE LAUGH

How is it that I'm able
To miss things I've never had,
And someone I've never met?

How can I look into the mirror
And miss memories I've never had,
And places we never went?

How can I lie here in bed
And miss arms I've never held
Or a laugh I've never heard?

And must I really wait through time
For you to show up one day
And make me feel less absurd?

SAY MY NAME

I once dated a boy who only listened to the instruments in songs,
He never heard the lyrics.
I should have known it wouldn't work out.
How is one that can't listen to words be expected to use them?
I memorize each line.

HOW TO RECOGNIZE REMORSE

I didn't recognize the regret,
      until it settled in the back of my throat
      like a stone.
Until I was shivering in a hot shower,
      rattling bones.
You said you'd forgiven me,
that there was nothing to forgive.
You smiled.
But all the world's a stage,
      and all the men and women
      merely players.
For all I know, it was a mask.
      God knows mine was.

CLOROX

What detox do I use
To cleanse myself of you?
What ties do I cut
To free you from my memory?

UNASKED

How is your life?
Now that we are finally separate,
Do you see me in the faces of other women
Like I see you in the footsteps of other men?
What are you doing?
Are you happy?
Did you find yourself ?

LONG TIME NO SEE

I thought I saw you
15 months later;
Slimmer waist,
Same stooped shoulders,
Smaller calves,
Same determined walk,
New confidence,
Same ease of movement.
I knew it was not you because this man's
Head was not so big.
But I searched and I searched,
Tried to look into your eyes and find
Your sadness through the window.
I panicked.
What if it was you?
I became grateful.
You had made it easy on me.
But it was strange;
15 months later
It was still not you.

AGE & GRACE

I realized I was getting old
When I could no longer sleep on my side
Without my hips aching in the morning
When a side pillow became a necessity
Instead of an accessory

When I honestly preferred podcasts to television
And early mornings to late nights
When my hips could pop with a single rotation
When I could no longer leave the house
Without forgetting something

When I said what was on my mind
Instead of what would ease yours
When I shared a bed and awoke with no regrets
When I left you and never came back

ODE TO A LOVER'S STRIFE

Like infant birds
My soul did wake
To soft landing words
That your lips did spake.

I knew you not at once
Nor what had begun
And the turbulence
That was soon to come.

Forsworn to another,
Mine were you not.
My curse as your lover:
To hold, but own not.

The tides did turn,
And the tables too,
And the light did burn,
She'd unveiled the truth.

But I'd loved you just
And you'd loved me true.
Alas, settled was the dust;
It was well worth the rue.

WISDO(N'T)M

I emerged unscathed
and that was when I knew
I was right.

I allowed you back
and that was when I knew
I was young.

I realized I deserved more
and that was when I knew
I was smart.

I did not demand it
and that was when I knew
I was learning.

TWO TYPES

There have been two types of men in my life:
– those who asked to read my words and
– those who never knew I wrote.

LONG DISTANCE RELATIONSHIPS & A FRENCH MAN

What if I said
I would cheat
If I thought you wouldn't leave me;
That I'm bored and alone,
And what's the harm in a one night stand?
He wouldn't be as good as you,
I may even say your name.
Maybe I could cheat just once…
Then I remembered masturbation.

SATISFACTION GUARANTEED

Sometimes I pretend I am my own lover
Looking in the mirror I tell myself the things
I have always wanted to hear
Praise my quirks as uniquely special
I am left speechless at the sight of the sparkle in my eyes
My courage inspires me
I find it endearing how guarded I am
But I will knock on the walls nonetheless
I know exactly what I need
And how to get it
I am the best lover
I have ever had

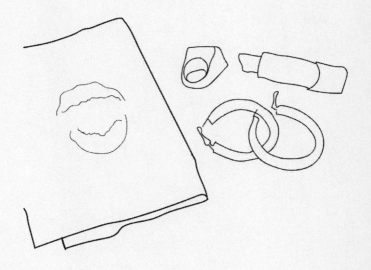

EIGHTY DEGREES AND PARTLY CLOUDY

I want you here so we can talk;
come over on Tuesday afternoon,
we can sit on the patio swing and stare out
at my dying grass and growing weeds.

You do not have to say anything.
I will apologize for yelling,
tell you I was not mad,
that I lied about the reason I left you,
explain that I still wonder if we could work,
tell you how complicated I am,
being with me is not easy.
I will be honest but not frank,
open and vulnerable.

I will tell you I was falling
and for all my bravery was afraid
you could not give me what I wanted.
I could not ask it from you anyway.

Secretly, I want you to tell me
you don't care,
it's okay,
you are ready to work.

But you will not.
You will be honest and open and vulnerable,
you will not veil how you feel.
I always loved that about you,
so I will let the sadness sit.

THINGS I THOUGHT I WANTED

I was content with my life
I'll have you know
But I wonder at my curious longing for things
That my youthful years couldn't know

I wanted someone to look at me
Like I was the sun
To be blinded and still marvel
And call me the one

I wanted someone to help me
Zip up my dress
To play love on my xylophone ribs
And make my hair a mess

I'd have loved a pair of strong hands
To hold me steady
To keep me anchored and sure
Until I'm ready

I wanted goofy melodramatic plays
At one in the night
Followed by soft butterfly kisses
At first sight of light

I wanted to make breakfast in bed
For one more than myself
And hand him the spare tools
As he attempts a bookshelf

I wanted to wake up to sleepy eyes
And muffled snores
And be content and sure in myself
Of a lifetime of mornings more

I wanted to share comfortable silences
As we read our own books
And talk through the easy silence
But swap looks

I know I'm a ridiculous person
I don't try to hide it
But I wanted someone who can laugh
Because he enjoys it

I wanted someone who finds me beautiful
Even when I'm not
Who could love me at my worst
And ease my tummy's knots

I wanted to share myself with someone
Who treasures the pieces
And have him share himself with me
Secrets told in morning breezes

And I wanted to see it all around me
The evidence of us:
Two toothbrushes, my reflection in his shirts
And in the sink, two coffee mugs

But adulthood moved in
Replacing the longing that was older than me
What did I know
I was only seventeen

My twenties taught me to want myself

RISING MAGMA

RISING MAGMA

This carefully crafted façade's
       Cracks grow bigger every day.
My carefully crafted smile
       Feels like it's painted on cracking clay.
No one looks at the cracks in a mountain's side,
       They only admire the view.
But the cracks scream a story;
       A volcanic eruption in the brew.

DETOX

I was 14, it was Black Friday
Blood between my legs
Refreshing
Her arrival
Tells me everything is alright
Things are in order
Who needs a juice cleanse when you can
Bleed it out?
For five days a month
Flush the tears
Drown the sorrows
Grab your chocolate
Bring your wine
Judgement-free bleeding
We were built for this
God knew we had too much on our plate
She gave us a week off

THE WIND STOPS FOR NAUGHT

The truth, though harsh,
flew wildly from my lips before I could tame it;
a habit I was known for,
in rage or in love,
but most often in both:
my greatest strength,
and my greatest weakness.

But I have decided —
it is better to speak the truth than allow it to be stolen.

VIOLET DELIGHTS

I took a walk to clear my mind,
left the house, buzzing with opinions,
        thoughts crashing within four walls.

I took a walk to clear my mind,
and the air tasted of lilacs and violets,
        and night pinks and purples,
        and smelled of sleepy roses.

A car passed by.
        Exhaust fumes.

I once read that humans ruin everything we touch,
including each other.
So I went back to those four walls.

POTENTIAL

In my early youth, I felt the constant need to explain myself.
In my later youth, I simply refused to.

DAWN

The brittle cold air
Momentary clarity
I breath it all in

WARM HUES

God spilled orange juice
She stained the blues with yellows
Sunset à la carte

REVOLUTIONARY

I'm a one man band
Heart hammering my ribcage
Can you hear me now?

NO ROAD MAP FOR LIVING

My therapist tells me I have time,
Time to choose.
There is always time.
She does not realize that it is not time
I am afraid of,
It is the choice itself.
Opportunities are beautiful,
Experiencing them is a blessing
But the choices are frightening;
There are too many options for failure.
So yes I have time, Jen.
Time to fail.

THE/RA/PY

Thinking to myself
as I book next week's session:
there is such a thing, you know,
as thinking too much.

HELLO DEPRESSION, MY OLD FRIEND

This blackness is ruthless,
A tyrant with an iron-fisted grip around my neck.
Soon my eyeballs will pop out
And my skull will house little more
Than grey matter, liquified,
Exiting in tiny streams through my ears.
The blackness is rattling me ragged
And is about two minutes away
From using my collar bones as drumsticks
And my phalanges as toothpicks.

This light, my little morsel of light,
Quivering and naked on my tongue
That tastes like hope,
Trapped behind my wired shut jaw
And my cemented teeth.
I think it snuck into my eyes too,
But in its timidity, hid behind my irises,
Not showing itself just yet.

I grow and become more complex in the world,
And my jigsaw puzzle of fears loses more pieces,
And I continually realize that
The monsters of this world,
Under my bed, or in the mirror,
Have nothing on loneliness.

SELF-CARE

You would be amazed
at the number of jokes I laugh at
by people I don't understand.

I have done things
I do not care about
for far too long.

PERSPECTIVE

Is that, there, heaven?
Through the big holes in the sky?
And is this, here, hell?

MATCH POINT

Lying on my back,
Staring down the big gray clouds.
Let's see who cries first.

LANDSLIDES

The rain fell and I did not allow myself to cry
And wondered why they called me cold.
In my efforts to be considerate
I destroyed more than I had saved.

PASSING CLOUDS

Suddenly tired, I looked up from my world,
realized it was not mine at all,
and smiled.

PAIN IS THE COLOR OF EGGPLANT

There's a bruise on my ankle
Like the dark rainbows of an oil spill.
The colors are pretty,
I've come to decide.

There's a bruise on my collarbone
Like the throbbing purples of eggplant.
Pain is the color of an eggplant,
I've come to believe.

There's a bruise on my heart,
Doesn't matter much how it got there.
I just have one now,
And the world didn't stop.

ROM COMS NEED NEW CHARACTERS

There is a difference between strength and safety.
Why do we fantasize the hiding of pain?

"She was suffering and no one knew it
And that was why she was beautiful."

Cry your tears,
Use my shoulder,
Support is not found unless sought for,
Support is not found unless offered.

The oppression of women will not end
Until our suffering is legitimized.

BLUES

The ocean and sky,
Two blue masses to drown in,
To choke, or to swallow.

MOOD SWINGS

The sky's mood has changed.
Blue curdled milk above me.
Everything's changed.

DISEASE

Trees rot from their roots
and fall in one piece.

GATHERING

Angry clouds approached,
Scissoring the sky in half.
Did we stand a chance?

REVITALIZE

It's okay to crack.
Tears are rain, let them cleanse you.
A new dawn awaits.

10:43 PM

I could feel the lights of the house wink out
one by one,
then the lights of the city all together,
and the sky wasn't the bruised
blue or black
the world had always told me
it would be.
It was the color of dull silver
in need of a good polish;
and this dull silver of a sky
started to throb with muted lightning,
a storm brewing miles away.

The boy and the bird I'd seen
in the silhouettes of the trees
started to move, talking to each other,
as the wind started to dance
through their branches.

The flowering bush outside my window,
long since overgrown,
had taken the form of an African woman
staring at me through my bedroom window,
with braids out of control.

Suddenly,
the dull silver wasn't throbbing but pulsing,
the lightning wasn't muted,
the wind wasn't dancing but howling.
Long gone were the boy and the bird,
and the braided woman was bent out of shape
by raving trees.

TANTRUMS & DIAMONDS

I just pointed a remote at the sky.
I tried to mute her thunderous sobs
But she wails on,
Throwing tantrums and moans.
I think she just threw her TV across the room,
I saw sparks fly.
Doors slam shut.
I do love her though.
She cries, and it's so beautiful.
It sounds bloody awful,
I will admit, but I enjoy the chaos too, on occasion.
Just not today.
But she's throwing up her diamonds that never seem to cut,
They simply melt into the grass
And into my hair.

STRUT

I often find myself stuck
between being strong and being honest
as if to show my real face
was to let someone down.
But is that not what we teach our daughters?
"Don't let them get to you,"
ignore the whistles,
stride through the glares.
It has become difficult for me
to admit that anyone has gotten to me,
for better or for worse.

I HAVE LEARNED SOME THINGS

I know many things
About the world,
About myself,
About how the world views myself.
It does not make me cocky to recognize these truths.
It does not make me arrogant to refuse to feign subtlety.
It makes me confident,
And that makes you uncomfortable.
I know that as well.

WORKING WOMAN

I want a job where I can drink wine at noon
Cook lunch at home and meet coworkers for happy hour
Wear Jimmy Choo and save the world
Be my own boss but have someone to drive me
Play by my own rules
In a way that satisfies others
I want a big office and big windows
But lots of privacy
I want your dependence on my
Independence
I want to be both
Feared and loved

SOLITUDE

Silence is my friend.
I keep myself company,
Sometimes too often.

WITHDRAWN

Painted my walls gray,
Seems more appropriate now,
Five birthdays later.

SORTING HAT

Ugly has its pros;
You can sieve through the people
Who really like you.

BARE

Trembling like a leaf,
Naked as the world stares on
And as I stare back.

NAKED

You didn't ask me to peel off my clothes or ask me to parade.
I did. For me.
It's exhausting having to hide a work of art
When all you want to do is show it off,
Like a Picasso under your bed.
What good is it there?
But I'm not offering this art of mine to you either.
Still mine.
Use only your eyes if you must.

Art galleries never offer you their art.
They don't let you hold the canvases.
They simply display it and tell you "That's all you get".
It's a two way street:
They get to breathe out, you get to breathe in.
This is that.

You don't get to touch me.
No one does. Not yet.
But you can admire,
And I can breathe.

SUN & MOON

SUN & MOON IN A SUITCASE

She asked me to describe
My favorite things,
To put them in a poem.

Words are lovely
They keep me nourished.
But for miracles like
Sunrises, or the moon,
Words are an ill-fitting suitcase:
Not nearly enough space,
Or nearly enough pockets.

So you jump on it,
And sit on it,
And desperately try to cram
As much in as you can.
And you try, you truly do.

But now you look down
And behold your handiwork:
Everything's squashed and creased,
And not nearly as beautiful
As when it had a sky for a home.

Who wants to be the girl
That suffocated the sunset,
Or the girl that shrank the moon?"

SANDSTORM

Staring towards the vastness of the ocean with my back to the world, I looked upon a great unknown. I felt like a speck of dust within a sandstorm, like the universe in all her superiority would swallow me whole. But the sandstorm is only as fierce as the grains of sand it accumulates; tiny as they may be, they are necessary, invaluable, to her cause. So I sat there, the dome of an ink blue sky above me curving down to meet the immense, deep bowl of ocean, seemingly insignificant. And I felt comfortable.

BONELESS BIRDS, STRINGLESS KITES

My thoughts are light-weighted souls;
      Boneless birds, stringless kites, helium balloons,
      Floating higher and higher,
      All but vanishing into the clouds.
The only way to pull them back into existence,
      To make them tangible,
      To keep them,
Is to write them down, just as I do now.
      Pen and paper
      Are the bones to my birds,
      And the strings to my kites.

STRANGERS ARE WE NONE

I delight
In the assumptions of strangers.
Yet strangers are we none
But mere souls,
Stitches of the same fabric,
Drops of the same ocean
Divided at birth,
Parted by a breath that promised reunion.

So we roam the earth,
Lead in the soles of our shoes,
Hope in the cavities
And strongholds of our chests,
And we tell ourselves
       "This may be the day.
       Perhaps it's today."

And suddenly, "one day" is today.
We may have traversed the world,
Lost ourselves in chock-full cities,
Found ourselves on desolate highways,
Perhaps forgetting the promise of our journey to begin with.
But finally, here we are: strangers.
Yet strangers are we none.

GOD AM I NONE

Beauty is perceived within the eyes of the beholder.
But so are the strange, the impossible, the time passed getting older.

What are these ghastly things, these creatures that look up in vain?
Are they codfish, swordfish, the fruits of my brain?

Colors not of this earth, shapes formed by no one but me.
Swishing forms from surface below; vision of a gray matter sea.

God am I none, to breathe life into these visions.
For my mind's offspring, *mes poisons*, remain on canvas and canvas alone.

LIGHT

I chase the light, and all she sends,
Her suns' and daughters' grace they lend.
Blind yellow beams slice me in half,
Gold shadows linger at my calf.
These windows stained, they beckon me
With prism smiles, religiously.
Darting eyes, by candlelight
At shadows grateful for their sight.
White rays caught in fractured places,
Spectrums creep across our faces.
And should I die before I wake,
Light, lead me home, hope, in my wake.

THE SUN SMELLS LIKE RAIN

The bench in the yard shines
Though cracked
Inviting but warning
If I lay here the bugs will cover me
There is a to-do list
But nothing for today

OUR WISHES

Every artist knows
We all have our own songs to sing
Like every child knows
The end of recess bell must ring.

But sometimes we still wish
Their song was the one we sung
Just like the child's wish
Is an extra minute before it's rung.

ON BEING A ROMANTIC FOR TWO HOURS

When the moon
Is big and bright enough
To paint shadowy humans
And watery trees.

When the moon
Is big and bright enough
To bleed more purple
Than black into the night void.

When the air is still
And I can hear the stringy whines
Of a guitar across the lake.
When the air isn't thick with thoughts.

It's a dull life to lead.
But for a couple hours
It's pretty nice.

EIGHTEEN GOING ON NINETEEN

A little sage once whispered in my ear
That new beginnings are nothing to fear.
In the end of something, comes another's mirth,
And from summer's death, came this autumn's birth.

So I propose a toast, to the misadventure,
To the sunrises, the rain dances, the walks ventured.
To the breezy golden leaves that waltzed above us,
To the seen and unseen magic that surrounded us.

And should you happen, beneath a night skylight's glass,
To see her bright orb and pinpricks of burning gas,
Take yourself back to this autumn; nineteen's lure.
To the evening bemusings with the girl next door.

SONGS FOR THE WRETCHED BULL

Have you taken the time lately
          To sit down and be truly honest?
To be rooted and still to the core of yourself,
          While the world's a spinning comet.
Are you at peace with your thoughts,
          Yet aware of your hunger?
Can you feel the seasons in you change,
          From winter, to spring, to summer?
Can you feel the buzzing and ringing in your ears,
          The urge to be alive,
But equally know how important it is
          To simply help everyone survive?
Can you admit to being lonely,
          Without forcing yourself to show it?
And can you delight in being silently happy
          And prove it just by glowing?
Are you willing to be two things at once,
          Or maybe just one thing?
Will you take the wretched bull by the horns
          And show it the songs it could sing?

SILVER

I always told myself I was going to leave to write
Cross an ocean to bring together words
But as I stared at the shadows the moonlight made
Against the gray walls I had painted myself
I realized I write the most
At home
Because while the moon is everywhere
It seems to shine the brightest through that window

MY AFRO FRAMES MY FACE LIKE A CLOUD

I used to believe in one love.
One love for one lifetime.
The fireworks of a teenage dream,
Zipping through the months,
But fading into dying years.

How much more wonderful
To sink in love with everything.
Fall in love with the vastness of the sky,
Drown in love with the gap-toothed smile of a stranger,
Dabble in the cynical humor of your best friend's boyfriend,
N'oublie pas d'aimer comment ta mère
       A t'aidé chaque soir avec ta français
With the children, smiles as big as Kampala,
      Running through the sprinklers.

Fall in love with Thomas' timidity in basketball,
      Despite being the tallest of them all.
With Michael who liked rap in foreign tongues,
      And held his hand to his hip as he did.
Fall in love with the ugliness of the world,
      With the smog that hides her curves.
      With the ugliness with which her mouth spits the truth.
Fall in love with her hills, her mountains,
      Her glacial peaks, before they all melt away.
Fall in love with her beauty.
      With the vulnerability with which she starts her days,
      Hoping in vain, that they end better than the last.

Fall in love with the little black boy,
  And the little white boy, whispering over a comic.
Fall in love with their belief that life will always be as wonderful.
Fall in love with the night,
  And all of her endless possibilities.
Fall in love with books,
  Lose yourself in the soft paperbacks,
  In the lives you can pretend to live, if only for an hour or two.
Fall in love with the stain glass windows,
  They cling to the reflections of rainbows.

Most importantly, fall in love with yourself.
Fall in love with yourself today, and tomorrow,
  And the day after that, and all the days that follow.
Mesmerize yourself with the way
  Your afro frames your face like a cloud,
The way your voice sounds in the shower,
  And the way your eyes go wide as the moon at a surprise.
Love your reflection every time you pass a mirror,
  And love her fiercely.
Love yourself and everything around you,
  Before you chase someone that could change their mind
tomorrow.

154

ACKNOWLEDGEMENTS

This book would not have been possible without the numerous people who shaped us, guided us, and cheered us on along the way. We would like to thank the following VIPs, though the list could go on forever.

Our families – for allowing us space to create, even when they were skeptical; and our mothers in particular who taught us time and time again that stubbornness could be a virtue.

Our husbands – for reading what we put in front of them and knowing when to get out of the way.

Sylvia and Marisha – for being our number one fans, for reading the first drafts, and for telling anyone who would listen that we were going to be published. We couldn't do this without your love and support.

The team at Eyewear Publishing / Black Spring Press Group, including our editor Cate Myddleton-Evans, for believing in us.

And to you, dear reader, for giving us a chance. We can't thank you enough.